The Rosary

of

Love

by ali ashraf

Preface

Love is indeed the strongest of human emotions. Human life begins with love when two bodies perform the act of physical love and conceive life, and human life ends with love too, when we cease to exist in physical form and submit our will to the will of an immense unknown force. But nowadays wherever I see, I see broken hearts, I see people hating love, I see hate overcoming. This might be because we as humans have become very selfish, more selfish than we naturally ought to be to survive. The reason for this, I believe, is our consumer-based capitalist economic system, which thrives on individualism, and to increase such individualism that can promote consumerist behaviour, this economic model has to make people selfish rather than selfless. The most powerful tool, however, to make people selfish, is a sexual pleasure with no strings attached.

Blind sex is an act solely based on self-pleasure, and an increase in such an act can lead to increase in selfishness as well, whereas love is purely a selfless act in which the lover just seeks to please the beloved regardless of any obstacles at hand. In love, the lover becomes completely selfless, but why so? Because love is nothing but complete submission of personal will. Because of the rapid disappearance of love, I see emptiness taking over human beings, I see humans fighting, I see nations fighting, I even see genders fighting. We have landed on the moon and made incredible advances, but we have forgotten to make a home for each other in our hearts. We have progressed a lot and this progress is making our lives full but our hearts are becoming empty. We see our colonies in space in the coming times, but we are unable to recover from the damage we have done to our Earth.

But still, I believe that human beings are made to love, they can't survive without love. If we take out love from our everyday social interactions, the entire humanity will collapse; a mother won't feed her child, a father won't educate his children, marital life will become solely based on sex, and this, unfortunately, is rapidly becoming the case.

Yet I still believe that however worse the situation may become, human beings will come back to love just like an angry child after crying for a long period comes back to his mother, rests his head in her lap, and falls asleep in content. To love when one is unloved is a saintly act, and to love with a broken heart is to fly with broken wings. The latter is almost impossible and a miraculous act, but once any soul learns to do that, then no obstacle can plant the seed of despair in that soul, it performs miracles that echo through history. Love will never lose, it will keep on finding its way into the hearts of mankind because love is the only thing that is without a cause, it just happens, it is the biggest act of divine intervention, the biggest proof of God's existence. It challenges the commonly established belief that everything follows a pattern, everything follows cause and effect, which is true except in the case of love, love is an exception to all rules.

Love and poetry are inseparable just like body and soul are inseparable and when separated they cause death. Yes, there can be poetry without love, but it is just like a body without a soul: cold, lifeless, and food for insects. In the same way, there can be love without poetry but it is just like a soul deprived of a body, floating amidst the heavens trying to find its place in the worldly realm, which in the case of love, it finally finds in the form of poetry. That is why I have chosen to write this poetry collection as a gesture to honour the most beautiful and strongest of human emotions i.e. love. We as humans must learn to love other human beings, we live in a strange time when people are fighting for animal rights but hurting other people, in such testing times, love must be our only anchor. I know that the world has become a cruel place and hope seems unreasonable, but human beings have a tendency to ignite hope even in the darkest of valleys, we have a tendency to breathe life into dead and empty deserts, but our only tool must be love and nothing else, so love love, for love is overcoming.

POEMS

you are the eternal ocean
of love and mercy
with infinite streams
bursting out of you
even if you give one drop
to the entire universe
the stars would sing in joy
and every creature will dance
in everlasting ecstasy
and all I ask for is a drop
from that drop.

(lost and found)

from where should I bring
a replacement of you?
my love, you are unique
in every possible way

I have lost myself
in search of you
and when I found you
I found myself

blessed is this losing and finding
in which nothing is lost
and nothing is found.

(at beloved's door)

O my heart!
what is this strange tune you play?
as upon the beloved's door, I lay
someday it'll open, waiting for that day
the day when all your hardships will pay

as mad as Majnun
I collect locks of beloved's hair
putting the pieces together with all the care
just to see my beloved again
whose one gaze will break this longing's chain

O my soul!
don't dwell in despair
we all know that one-day beloved will be here
we know our journey and we know our way
let the things be as they stay

O sweetness of longing!
you burn within, the desire of seeing
and being one again and all of your pain
won't go in vain
in the end, what you want, you will gain

there's ecstasy in both
parting and meeting
one is fuel, the other is fire
I love both, for both are the gifts
of my beloved; my only hope, my only desire

I know one day the door will open
I will finally see the face
the face that is the sun
of my moon's light
the face that is the source
of my grace.

(laughter)

even if that smile
doesn't shine now
in the nights of my misery

I can still hear
the echo of that laughter
illuminating my soul.

these distances won't
break me down
and I know someone
maybe around
but you know it too
you are mine
and I know our love
will be found
although I know I am
so far away
seems impossible for us
to meet today
but honestly let me say
that I don't know about you
but my love will
forever stay
and be the same
for my heart gets drunk
at the mention of your name
just let me rest my head
upon your lap
then the purpose of my creation
will be attained.

(midnight prayers)

Oh, my Lord!
my midnight prayers
are filled with tears

my strength is weakening
my body has become frail
I need ointment for the scars
that longing has left on my heart

I pray for mercy and grace
I pray for forgotten days
I pray for friends long gone
I pray for life forlorn

bring joy to all the lovers
let union be their fate
let them rejoice,
give them wings
so they could fly
and kiss each other's feet.

why have I become drunk
inhaling this air?
it must have touched
your intoxicating hair
and all its tresses

now I remember
before coming to my land
this winter breeze
it passes through
your breath so sweet
before my home, it passes.

(only love)

love came and took everything from me
now only love is left in me
and only love I see
only love I pray, only love I say
only love I hear, only love every day
now just one remains, not two
only love is here, neither me nor you.

I have left those days behind
when instead of the sun
your smile used to shine
when you were mine
I have left those days behind.

(tomorrow)

O my beloved!
you are the only spring
that my heart has ever known
I yearn and long to witness again
the spring of my soul
that your face brings
and the blooming of my soul
as you come along
but alas! this waiting, it never ends
ask me how many tomorrows
I have seen
and how many tomorrows
are long gone
yet that tomorrow
has never come
that will bring my love along.

13

where's my sunshine?
where's my moon?
where are my stars?
what is this strange hour?
where's that time gone?
when things were ours
now everything is yours
even me
ah! how time has flown
and how it flies to the unknown
journey of souls, how I long
to see your face
that at nighttime shone
just for once
say "come"
and I'd say anon.

(when everything is lost)

wherever love starts to grow
there nothing else remains
only love can be seen
no mirth and no pain

the storm of love came
took everything from me
I felt like a straw of hay
in love's mighty storm

love is the reason
this universe exists
without love, there can't be
no matter, no form

love is eternal
love will never die
when everything is lost
love will suffice.

(in the end)

15

wherever love sets its foot
there nothing remains at all
no spring can be seen in sight
a constant autumn, a constant fall

love carelessly keeps
both worlds
under its feet
no one can ever escape its thrall

intellect fails
reason cannot prevail
when love projects itself
on the heart's wall

against the strong winds
of fiery love
no one can stand firm
no one can stand tall

only love will remain
in the end
when all else is gone

once and for all.

(be gone)

leaves don't have
a will of their own
they go wherever
they are blown

the will of the wind
becomes their will
if the wind becomes still
they become still

be like leaves, my friend,
don't be a stone
with the fiery blows of wind
be gone!

(the unborn)

love affirms all negation
love is the master of all creation
love is beyond all stations
love is silence, love is noise
love is foolish, love is wise
love brings light to the darkness
love brings darkness to the light
love is evil, love is pure
love is less, love is more
love is hidden, love is shown
love begets and stays unborn.

(I am there!)

19

where all is music
where everything is beautiful
where flowers are always blooming
where all times are springtime
where autumn is spring
where without is within
where nymphs are singing hymns
where differences are akin
where nothing is a sin
where lovers always win
I am there!

20

your touch raises
a thousand storms within me
I am lost within you
when you are lost within me.

(fire of love)

fire! fire! light the fire
the night is closing in.
the night is close
and we're alone
the fire we will need

light the fire, light the fire
it'll give us needed warmth.
amidst the night
and in the dark
we'll warm our tired arms

light the fire, light the fire
our companion it will be.
the night is long
we're not at home
desires will extinguish

light the fire, light the fire
that will bring into our sight,
the things we know
but never saw
for it will bring us light.

light the fire, light the fire
that will burn our fragile hearts
we'll be done
in the blink of an eye
for this fire is divine

light the fire, light the fire
it will burn every desire.
I know you're tired
I know we are tired
let's light this holy fire.

(put me at rest)

you, placing your hand on my chest,
have taken away my last breath
my soul is your captive now
my world within your palms rest

ah! come again, once again
for I am lost within the shine of your eyes
come, so I can breathe again
come, bring me back to life

this parting has torn me since
you were here, I've last seen you
now where lies peace for my heart?
nowhere expect within your embrace

how will I live this long life?
without a heart within my chest
just for once come back to me
come and put me at rest.

(melancholia)

24

adorned in melancholy
I am sleepless at midnight
occupied by your thoughts
my eyes shed tears
and I make a necklace
from those pearls
to hang myself
to sacrifice myself for love

your love has made me wither
I have lost all wishes
and my tendency to wish
is it human? is it sane?
is it moral? is it humane?
I am beyond questions now
I don't want answers
I just want to weep tirelessly
and repeat your name
all night long
as I am adorned
in melancholia,
sleepless and tired.

(I love you)

O owner of my soul!
source of my being
keeper of my secrets
take off all my skin
one by one
then cut my body into pieces
one by one
spill my blood on the streets
one by one
then burn those pieces into flame
one by one
then gather the ashes of those pieces
one by one
and scatter those ashes in the air
one by one
you would still hear me say
I love you.

(our home)

I belong somewhere beautiful
among beautiful people
where the language is poetry
where roses sing in praise
where crystal clear rivers flow
where the sun doesn't burn
where the moon is always full
and where you and I
sleep in each other's arms
all night long under the full moon
where morning breeze brings joy
where there is no work at hand
where love is the only currency
where eyes sprinkle with happiness
where there is no fear
where there are no laws of nature
neither human laws to adhere
where it's neither so cold or hot
where things do not rot
where hearts speak and tongues listen
where all lovers live in communion
that place never existed
that place might never exist

but when I close my eyes
I see it as our home
and I am filled with joy.

(being polite)

you lighted up my world
like a spark for a while,
how unfortunate I was
I thought the day had arrived.
I mistook you for the sun
that was me being naive,
you burned my world and said
"I was just being polite".

(spring)

my soul wants to dance
but it is trapped in a cage
I see the sunset every day
I think about my passing age
with each day gone
I have not grown
but only withered
I wish you to breathe on me
and put a new life in me
my soul's garden has seen many falls
now it craves a spring
that'll bring back the innocence
and I'll smile like a baby
in his mother's arms
I crave a spring that'll forever last
my hopes have grown old
my feet have become sore
in search of you
please do not hide from me anymore
O love of my existence!
shake me, so my withered leaves
could fall altogether at once
and make room for a new spring

where I belong in your arms.

(being you)

you are in my heart
like a pregnant woman
carries a child in her womb
you never part from me
you are ever-growing
you have taken over me;
my body, my soul
my heart, my bones
my blood, my veins.
now you flow through me
I no longer know myself
I am you
I was never me
it was a deception
I was born drunk
I will die drunk
in your eternal ecstasy
of being you.

(ecstasy)

there's no need to bring
the wine in a goblet
for I am so much drunk
seeing those eyes
and I lost my senses
and lost my sight
all I could see is ecstasy
all I hear is ecstasy
all I could say is ecstasy
all I wear is ecstasy
and since I have worn
this love's hair shirt
I put skewers in my eyes
and put my head in dirt
yet the immense beauty
doesn't stop to overcome me
and I live in ecstasy
I breathe in ecstasy

she lifted her brow
and the universe stood still
what a sight to see!

(your grave)

there are many graves
in my heart
but yours is the most beautiful
of them all.

(except you)

I have travelled a thousand miles
covered myself in thousand styles
kissed the sand and touched the wind
loved and been loved akin
embraced the good and yes, I've sinned
lose sometimes and sometimes I win

one thing I've learned
from the journeys made
by becoming a jack
of all trades
by having scars of journeys on my skin
by letting new experiences in
yes, I've learned this thing for sure
nothing is worth living for
except your eyes
except your love
except your smile
except your touch.

(eternal romance)

Oh, how sweetly you move inside me
it tingles my entire being
I get overcome by ecstasy
and become drunk without drinking
the stars dance along with me
in a state of trance
O my sweet love!
if I get a chance
I'll forever stay in this state
and become one with you
in this eternal romance.

(gold and dust)

whoever is touched by love
either becomes gold
or turns to dust
in the eyes love
both are same
both are worth it
both are one

(somebody tell me)

although I've burned
all of your pictures
but how should I burn
what's imprinted on my heart?
even though it's burning.
although I've forgotten
what you said
but how could I forget
and peel off my skin
that has your memory
like blood stains
living all over it
bleeding time by time?
how could I undo
what's already done?
how could I walk
with broken bones?
that call your name
with each crack
and I know that I can't
live with you anymore
but how could I live
with this traitor

that beats inside me
still calling out your name
every single day?
how do I live
with myself anymore?
somebody tell me
how to live
all alone and forlorn.

(all over me)

although it's been many days
since you left
but I can still smell
your sweet fragrance
roaming around me
filling the air
I can still feel
your warm breath
on my skin
I can still feel
your arousing touch
and when I touch
the parts you've touched
I fall in love with myself
for I still have your presence
imprinted all over me.

(poetry flows)

when I see you
poetry flows.

42

I see you
in every tear, I shed
in every promise I break
in every love story's end
in every flower that blooms
in melancholy glooms
in every thorn that hurts
when my eyes are shut
I see you in myself
when I am no longer myself
I see you.

(light)

my friend needed light
so, I burned myself
to light up his nights
and make his days bright

44

your love has peeled off my skin
and burned me at stake
I no longer exist
except in sweet pain

(moonlight)

under the moonlight
she shines bright
as if she is the moon
and moon seeing her sight
becomes drunk.

(dream)

between the state of sleep
and wakefulness
I see you
with half-closed eyes

(tender)

every single hair of my body
becomes filled with ecstasy
when with your tender fingers
you touch me

(in love with myself)

I kiss my heart every day
cause you live in it
I am in love with myself
cause I am the one who loves you
nothing can take me away from you
except you, when you take my breath away.

(enamoured)

amidst the darkness
there comes a light
as my soul is enamoured
by the glow of your memories.

touch every single part of my body
set me on fire with your embrace
let me melt in your arms
let me be lost in your grace

a thousand flowers bloom in my body
with your one-touch
and when you brush my hair with your fingers
my entire body yearns
for more of you
for the love of you
for the touch of you

you become one of me
I become one of you
we shun duality in a blink
and become drunk in each other
as this love's wine, we drink.

(break it with care)

my heart is fragile
break it with care
so this immense pain
I might learn to bear.

52

Is there a maiden so fair
no one touched or laid eyes on?
that I can hold in my arms
and forever call my own?

(life goes on)

look at the stars and their motion
look at the clouds as they depart
the message that nature whispers
into every human's heart
is clear as the bright daylight
that nothing forever lasts

so, this tale goes
of a girl's woes
as her life changed
as she heard the news
of the passing of a fair young man
whose eyes were her rescue
where she lost herself carefree
and bid the worries adieu

alas! but as the happy times
are nothing but a spring
and like the changing seasons
she had autumn within
her only spring was gone
the face of her beloved
and now she was all alone

but all times have to passes
sorrows also don't last
again the springtime came
and along it brought
a beautiful face
a handsome young man
forwarded his hand
and all her sorrows
disappeared in his glance.

(she)

her eyes are deeper than the ocean
she sets all things in motion
her one smile shuns misery in a glance
and the universe dances under her trance.

under the sun
she smiled
and the sun
turned bright.

(woman)

sun bathes in her eyes
moon glistens in her tears
world rejoices in her laughter
universe whispers in her ears.

(last night I)

last night
he and I were all alone
he touched every single hair of my body
and every single particle of my soul
became enamoured within his thrall

last night
we talked all night long
beneath the moonlight as it shone
over us lover's faces
and we whispered all night long
in each other's ear
I became his secret and he became mine
such was the ecstasy of our meeting
last night.

(love's fragrance)

59

fumed
fragrance far
from imagination's grasp
fills the life's emptiness
flowers the spring amidst fall.

(true love)

a madman doesn't need to wander
in jungles and desert sand
he carries the raving madness
within his chest, within himself

his shirt torn, his heart ripped
his eyes shedding tears of blood
his repute lost, his senses gone
he stands there proclaiming to be a god

such is the ecstasy of true love
such a state of a lover can be
he wanders seven heavens within a glimpse
and puts the universe under his feet.

I want to lose myself
in desert, in jungle,
lost in your thought
repeating your name
like an old woman
recites her rosary,
until I start to lisp
and my tongue becomes tired

I want to cry
in your longing
until my throat starts to ache
and stops making a sound.

O my beloved!
I have never seen
such a grace
that your face holds.
don't test me more
let us merge and be one
and become careless
about this trembling empire
called "the world".

62

love is
to set yourself on fire
and not care

love is
to turn to ashes
and rise again

love is
to grow wings
while crawling

love is
to write on the wind
with kisses

love is
indescribable
yet books are filled with it.

(once lost)

as we neared
to feel
the spark again

as we neared
to have
the touch again

as we neared
to witness
the ecstasy

as we neared
to set
ourselves free

we came to know
it will be found again
what we once lost.

(you are the only one)

the sound of that laughter
still echoes in my empty life even after
it's been so long that it has been gone
don't cry my poor heart
instead, be brave and strong
you are the only thing I've left,
you are the only one I've got.

(fire and water)

life is fire, love is water
one burns, the other extinguishes
but they both can never be one
one must end for the other to exist.

(voice)

in the nights of despair
a voice echoes
illumines my soul
brings joy to the darkness

that voice is yours, my friend,
that voice is yours.

(eternity)

if you have not loved
you have not lived
if you have loved
you will never die

(slavery of love)

68

your love has taken over my soul
like a merciless king
I am at your mercy now
your eyes have enslaved me
your arms captivated me
the tresses of your hair
have chained my feet

what a beautiful slavery it is
If the world ever has
the slightest taste of it
they wouldn't think twice
and gamble their freedom for it.

(indescribable)

how should I tell about
the beauty of my beloved?
when I do, I stammer and stutter
with excitement.
alas! how I am rendered helpless
and speechless,
that beauty cannot be described
in words confinement.

(beatific vision)

70

I hear the voice of the voiceless.
I see the face of the faceless.
people say I am a raving madman
for I kiss upon the passing breeze
thinking of it as your feet.

you have taken
the world away from me
and made me only yours
for that I love you
and hate you both.

(love letter)

this love letter that I write
with the pen of sigh
the ink of tears
I send it at midnight
through the wind -
this cool summer breeze
to a faraway place
of your abode
which is far from my reach.

(drunk)

I can feel the heat
in my blood
a fragrance
in my sweat
drunkenness
in my head
carelessness
in my speech
shiver
in my body

since I saw you
last night.

the kisses you gave me
on my naked body
turned into jasmines
and showered fragrance everywhere,
the universe bowed to me in love
I embraced it with tears
and fell in love with myself.

(shooting stars)

if you desire
I will catch the shooting stars
with my hands
and turn them into candles
for you to shine.

in every face
I see you.

(black and white)

all colours have faded
my life is black and white
without you.

(I have become you)

lost in you
I ceased to exist
I don't love you
I have become you.

I can feel the sunshine in my heart
I can feel my soul torn apart
and rivers flowing from it
when I see you

I can hear the fairies singing songs
and the nightingale sings along
Oh, I waited for so long
just to see you.

(dervish I)

80

when I see your beauty
my heart becomes restless
I cry tears of joy
and shout with carelessness

my love, your love
has given me
pleasure in pain
my tears don't
go in vain
they grow wings and fly
and touch the seven skies.

my soul dances
to a secret tune
that has its source
in your heart.

write your name
on my body
with kisses
and make it permanent
with your fiery breath.

83

the glow of her face
puts moon to shame,
the shine in her eyes
is more than starry nights.

if you feel
you are flying
without wings
you are in love.

(symphonies)

a million beautiful symphonies
play at once
when you smile.

(soulmate)

in love,
the entire universe
is your soulmate
you don't have to
find one.

(soul's flight)

if body flies
it's miracle
if soul flies
it's love.

from fiery lavas of venus
to the sparkle of moon dirt
from intense meteor showers
to helium on the sun,
only love is worth discovering
only love deserves to be heard.

(all night long)

you have robbed me
of sleep,
I hear the moon whispering
songs in my ear,
I see the stars rejoice and dance
under trance,
all alone, all night long.

90

last night
when you touched me
my tears became fire
they have ignited new life in me
I do not worry anymore
I have become careless and carefree
I dance like a child
and play in mud all-day
not caring what people think
I feel my soul spin
I feel a flame within
since you touched me
last night.

(maybe)

maybe my heart
will stop beating for you
when it will stop beating
altogether.

(pain of love)

I want to feel
pain of your love
in my body
and blazing fire
of your breath
in my soul.

(the touch of love)

your touch sets me on fire
I, overcome by desire,
bleed tears of joy
and when you hear my cry,
a sweet ecstasy runs
through my veins
what I feel is beyond
description and names.

(acid of love)

your love throws
burning acid
on my already
open wounds
yet I smile
and laugh
to please you.

(kiss)

give me all your secrets
through a passionate kiss
then sew and seal my lips
with your fingertips.

(the ocean)

you awakened the poet in me
my soul was calm in a soundless sleep
the tumult of your love
brought forth tears of blood
I have become all alone
in this wide wild world.

(where lovers meet)

I want to meet you
in a place
where lovers meet

a place beyond the fabric
of time and space
a place where there's no
night or day

a place that is known
only to our eyes
a place that will live
eternally in our sight.

(the illusion)

what a stupid man
was I
what a beautiful illusion
you were.

(angelic face)

show me your angelic face
for I want to lose my senses
my sanity is of no use
if it's not lost on you.

(dervish II)

100

the light of your love
has entered my heart
it has illuminated my soul
it has given me wings to fly
I travel the entire universe
in the blink of an eye.

(mercy)

my chest is torn apart
and the ocean of love flows
through my heart
I bathe in its pure
sparkling water
under moonlit allure
I see the colours
that were present
yet never apparent
I feel the love
that was present
but never felt.

(intimacy)

deep ocean eyes
long slender thighs
a touch that melts
between burning legs
pain starts to please
time begins to cease
passion all night
hot fiery sighs
bodies oppress
against each other press
you look me in the eyes
with moans of joy
tongues twist kiss
fists grab wrists
pleasure continues
hands stray loose
on bodies pained yet wet
that start to sweat
pleasure overcomes
we shake as one
and all that is done
that seems forbidden.

(lovers cry)

let us put our arms
around each other
and melt into oneness
through embrace
let us cry
on each other's shoulders,
be overcome by grace

then talk about separation
and in oneness cry
then talk about oneness
and in separation cry.
let us cry all night long
with each other along
let us cry in misery
let us cry in joy.

(leaf)

I am a leaf
light and helpless
in your love's storm
since I fell from my branch
I wander and roam
I find no peace at all
I have no home
take me wherever you want
never leave me alone.

love is the only
harmonious melody
all else is just
chaos and noise.

(february)

flowers bloomed in ecstasy
as came the month of february
life sprung out of death
as lovers, in february met.

(luminous)

last night
the moon descended
into my soul
bathed in it
then rose
the next morning
as the sun.
I feel grace everywhere.

(embrace)

we cried on each other
in embrace
while we saw each other
from faraway.

(love is overcoming)

109

there's no book of love
yet all books talk of love
love is untouched yet felt
love is unsaid yet heard
love is not taught yet learned
love is not learned yet known
love is a thirsty flame
love is an arrant knave
love is secret of all secrets
love is beyond all mysteries
love is an all-knowing king
love is what nightingale sings
love is what is known in spheres
love is what kills without care
love love, for love is only worth loving
love love, for love is overcoming.

Please leave a review to support.

Instagram: aliashraf_poetry

Other Books by Ali Ashraf:

- The Divine Tavern
- JAZB: Urdu Poetry With English Translation
- Invocations: Islamic Sufi Poetry Collection
- Sad But Not Depressed: Sad Love Poetry Collection
- Redemption: Emotional Poetry about God, Jesus, and The Bible Prophecies